T0354716

REINCARNATION

Dr. Z. Gilead

REINCARNATION

iUniverse books may be ordered through booksellers or by contacting:

iUniverse
1663 Liberty Drive
Bloomington, IN 47403
www.iuniverse.com
844-349-9409

ISBN: 978-1-6632-6977-5 (sc)
ISBN: 978-1-6632-6978-2 (e)

Library of Congress Control Number: 2024927141

Print information available on the last page.

iUniverse rev. date: 12/30/2024

Contents

BOOK 1

Why do we need to study Reincarnation - the last and greatest mystery of our lives

I had long been intrigued by reincarnation and life after death. My interest in the subject was stimulated by watching on television the funerals of hundreds of Israeli soldiers who died in the Hamas/Hezbollah-Israeli war, and by grieving for the many tens of thousands of Gaza strip citizens and their children dead by the unintentional actions of Israeli soldiers and pilots - forced by the difficult war against the ambushes of Hamas terrorists and their explosive devices.

But my interest was mostly energized by the billions of men, women and children dead because of cancer, Flu, fever, Pneumonia, Alzheimer and other pestilences of our times. **Alas, Humanity is ephemeral!**

During archaic times, the lifespans of Humans were about 25-35 years. In modern times, **Hurrah!** Humans managed to reach 35-60 years of age. Happily, most recently, with the advent of Modern Medicine, we may even reach one hundred years. But, even in the most recent long lifespans mentioned, Humanity is losing large stores of knowledge and experience!!! Imagine a

Newton or an Einstein or various Nobel prize winners with very long lifespans, and with all their faculties intact!!!

As a result, for my own consolation, and mostly for the consolation of numerous grieving people, I decided to write on **reincarnation**. Possibly, because of putative reincarnation, Humanity may continue to progress and "live" after death in other realms - in far-away planets?...

For writing the present book, I googled for stories of reincarnation. In these stories, many lay people claimed that they underwent a partial or complete reincarnation.

If reincarnation exists, then it should be heralded by all the world's religions. This could bring considerable consolation to all mourners. Unfortunately, most of the discussions of religious servitors with grieving people deal only with the demise of the physical body. There are barely any discussions on reincarnation. When religious servitors try to console mourners, they talk mostly about the five stages of mourning (Kobler-Ross), and they stress mostly the fifth stage of mourning (acceptance). We cannot blame them, because the esoteric idea of reincarnation, unfortunately, does not receive any wide publicity in our "scientific" world although numerous physicians support it.

BOOK 2

Scientific and medical proofs
for Reincarnation and NDE
(near death experiences)

Many physicians and scientists believe in the existence of reincarnation and some of their studies are brought below. The scientists and medical people even state that reincarnation is not only possible, but is also a mundane, daily occurrence. Some of their reports on reincarnation is brought here

Aside from complete "terminal" reincarnation, many people experience NDEs – near-death experiences. These are experiences that happen during near-death. They are short experiences that happen to people who have died and had been successfully resuscitated.

Interestingly, the Druze secret religion and some eastern religions do believe in reincarnation after death. The Druze people tell stories about children who revealed the locations of treasures hidden by their ancestors who died before they could divulge the location of these treasures to their families.

In addition, there are many reports of people who went in print to claim that they, personally, underwent partial reincarnation during NDE (near-death experiences).

The following is a stirring report that was brought by several reporters and has been investigated by a state- appointed committee:

The life and reincarnation story of Shanti Devi

"Shanti Devi was born on the 11th of December 1926, in New-Delhi, India. As a little girl, when she was about four years old, she started to tell her parents that she had memories of her previous life, and that her "real" home is in the city of Methura, and that is where her husband lives. Methura is 145 kilometers from her New-Delhi home.

As expected, her parents ignored her story. Not getting any response, at the age of six years, she ran from home to reach Methura by herself. When she failed, she started to tell her friends at school that she was a married woman, became pregnant and died 10 days after giving her husband a boy.

Her teacher and the school's principal tried to dissuade her, but noticed as they talked to her, that she used names and words in the dialect of Methura which she had never heard before. In her talk, she disclosed the name of her previous wheat-merchant husband: "Kadr-Nath".

The principal made inquiries. and located in Methura a wheat-merchant who answered to this name and whose wife, named "Lodge Devi", died ten days after the birth of a son.

Perplexed, Kadr-Nath himself traveled to Shanti's house in New Delhi and pretended to be his brother. Shanti immediately identified him and their son who came with him. When she was taken later to Methura, she also described intimate details about Kadr-Nath's life with her. As a result, Kadr-Nath was sure that Shanti Devi was indeed a reincarnation of his late wife. After Shanti recognized him, he disappeared. He was ashamed because he promised Shanti on her deathbed that he would never marry again. This he did not fulfill…

When Mahatma Gandhi, then India's spiritual leader, heard about the case, he sent a committee to investigate Shanti's claims.

5

The committee's members used several tricks to verify Shanti's claims. For instance, they drove with her to Methura and indicated some house there as her family's house. But Shant told them to continue driving and identified her previous house. When in Methura, Shanti identified a number of relatives from her earlier life, including her grandfather.

One committee's report was published in 1936, and then another one in 1952. These reports were based on interviews carried out with Shanti and her Methuran relatives. The committee decided, unanimously, that she is indeed a reincarnation of the late Lodge Devi.

After her visit to Methura, Shanti returned to her family home in New Delhi and lived there. Shanti never married.

She told her story several times. In her last interview with one reporter, she recounted her **life's end experience** and that it was terrible to die and then reincarnate. Shanti was also interviewed by a Swedish author who published in 1994 a book about her life.

One reporter continued to meet with Shanti. Their last interview took place on 27th of December 1987, four days before her death.

Bibliography:

Guy wright: "The life of Shanti. A story on a little girl and Reincarnation". "Mako", March 11, 2020.

Bubriski: "Shanti Devi – an Indian story about reincarnation who shocked the whole world". "Tube". October 1st, 2021.

The studies of Dr. Long – trying to Understand Near-Death Experiences (NDEs)

Dr. Long is a foremost proponent of NDEs. As already described above, NDEs are experiences of transient, near-death-reincarnations. Dr. Long wrote a book in which he declared: "I have studied more than 5,000 cases of near-death experiences. My research has convinced me, without a doubt, that there is reincarnation after death."

Dr. Long's explorations started while in medical school. At that time, he stumbled across an article describing NDEs in "The Journal of the American Medical Association". The article stirred his curiosity so much, that on his graduation from the medical school, he decided to study NDEs, and established a foundation for their study. With incredibly meticulous assembly-techniques and analysis of accounts, Dr. Long was able to uncover a collection of experiences that defy current conventional understanding. These experiences, whether taking place during clinical death, or in life-threatening situations, demonstrate common phenomena that indicate that there is existence after death.

After finishing residency in radiation oncology, Dr. Long practiced in a hospital affiliated to the University of Iowa. Early in his medical career the wife of one of his friends told him a detailed story about her experiences after her heart stopped under anesthesia. Her account stirred him a lot and drove him to study NDEs. While working as a physician in Las Vegas, Dr. Long was influenced by medical people who had invited him to a series of lectures by Raymond Moody, a physician and a noted NDE researcher.

Dr. Long established his Near Death Experience Research Foundation (NDERF) in 1998. The foundation maintains a website, also launched in 1998, and a database of more than five thousand cases. This is the world's largest collection of near-death reports. In 2014, the NDERF calculated that, on an average, 774 NDEs happen each day in the United States.

Dr. Long had asserted that the most common terms used by people to describe what they felt during their NDE experiences were "peacefulness-" and "love-" feelings.

Dr. Long wrote a book entitled "Evidence of the Afterlife: The Science of Near-Death Experiences", which became a New-York-Time Best Seller. He had also appeared in many media outlets. Dr. Long also contributed to "The handbook of near-death experiences: thirty years of investigation" which was published by Praeger In 2009. The book is a comprehensive critical review of research carried out within the field of near-death studies and is considered to be an important publication in the field. Its thirteen chapters range from a scholarly review of the published evidence to discussions of the theory of consciousness, up to personal accounts by physicians of their own near-death experiences. All the authors of the book, except one author, were physicians and scientists. This increases the objectivity of the reports since they were made by scientifically trained observers.

There have been additional published studies of NDE in recent medical literature. To wit: Dr. Pim Van Lommel, Md. from the Nederland, described a prospective multi-hospital study of cardiac arrest patients who experienced NDE.

Modern interest in NDEs dates back only from about fifty years. But descriptions can be found from the ancient Greeks: Heraclitus, Democritus, and Plato all wrote on "revenants" - people who died and then recovered.

While the existence of NDEs is recognized, they are not understood. Dr. K. Nelson, a neurologist, argued that NDEs should be placed within modern neuroscience. Other authors deny this. E. Alexander, a neurosurgeon, makes an equally compelling argument for placing NDEs **outside of the framework of Neuroscience**. His argument revolves around the theory of consciousness (a state of being aware of something within oneself). He says that the consciousness of NDEs is produced by the brain as a sort of epiphenomenon - a secondary mental phenomenon accompanying another one and caused by it. Therefore, it should not be included in neuroscience.

Still, several experts strongly state that physicians should recognize NDEs as being part of the life experience of at least some of the patients.

Many people who have had such NDEs feel a need to talk about them. Most are affected by their NDEs. While NDEs are positive and happy experiences, some may be negative or threatening. NDE has also caused some cases of PTSD (post-traumatic stress disorder).

Anyway, NDEs should induce in all of us a feeling of humility: For all the knowledge and skill of neurologists and consciousness experts, there are things which we do not yet understand.

Let Shakespeare have the last word:

> *"There are more things in heaven and earth, Horatio, Then are dreamt of in your philosophy".* (Hamlet 1.5.167-8), Hamlet to Horatio).

Reference:

1. Van Lommel P, van Wees R, Meyers V, Effect I. "Near-death experiences in survivors of cardiac arrest: A prospective study in the Netherlands." Lancet. 2001; 358:2039–45.

Reports on persons' feelings during NDA

A research team examined the language written by terminally ill cancer patients as documented in blog posts of their final days. The team compared the words of these cancer patients' words to the language of healthy participants. All were asked to imagine what it would be like to feel as if they were dying.

The healthy participants used negative language, including words like "anxiety," "fear," and "terror." Meanwhile, the terminally ill patients, or death-row criminals, used **a more positive language, such as "love" and "happiness."**

In a second experiment, the research team analyzed the last words of death-row inmates and compared them with the words of non-inmates who were asked to imagine what facing imminent death would be like.

Again, the results were similar. The words of the death-row inmates were much more positive than those of the non-inmates.

A personal note from the author

I had a beloved brother who was extremely ill. He suffered from a brain tumor and finally languished, comatose, for several weeks in a hostel. I and my sister visited him every day. In his last day of life, he woke up and his face lit up with a beatific smile (this is the only way I can define it). Over the night he passed away…

BOOK 3

An exposition (treatise) on reincarnation as viewed by various religions and lay people

How do the Major Religions View the Afterlife?

Despite all their diversity of beliefs, the major religions are in accord in one great teaching: Human beings are immortal, and their spirits came from a divine world and eventually will return to this world as the result of reincarnation. Unfortunately, as I already indicated above, in practice, most of the discussions of religious servitors with mourners, deal only with the death of the physical body. There are barely any discussions on reincarnation. This way, unfortunately, they cancel the great promise and hope that religions could offer to their followers, if they had discussed the possibility of reincarnation. The promise of reincarnation could counter the assertions of materialists who say that there is no afterlife, and that death is the end.

The Neanderthals (circa 100,000 b.c.e.) often covered their dead with red pigment. They also placed food, stone implements, decorative shells and bones in the graves. Obviously, there are no written scriptures describing the purpose of including such funerary objects in the graves (Writing was not invented until the fourth millennium B.C.E). Therefore, we can only assume that the placement of weapons, food, and other utilitarian items beside the dead indicates that these prehistoric people believed that death was not the end. They probably assumed that a tribesman who was no longer among the living, still required nourishment, clothing, and protection to journey safely in another kind of existence beyond the grave. Somehow, they believed that there was some part of the buried persons that survived death.

Similarly, anthropologists can only guess whether the earliest members of the Homo sapiens species (circa 30,000 b.c.e.) conducted burial rituals of a quality that would qualify them as religious. It is known that they buried their dead with care and consideration and included in their graves food, weapons, and various personal belongings.

That part of the Human being that survives death is known in Christianity, Islam, and Judaism as "the soul," - the very essence of the individual person that must answer for its earthly deeds, good or bad. All the major world religions hold the belief that the way a person has conducted himself or herself while living on Earth, will influence his or her soul's ultimate destiny after physical death.

Many teachings state that the only reason for birth into the material world is the opportunity to prepare for the soul's destiny in the immaterial world. The teachings state that the manner a person will meet the challenges of life, how he chose to walk - in the path of good or evil - will determine how his soul will be treated after death. All the seeds that one has sown throughout his or her lifetime, good or bad, will be "harvested" in the afterlife.

Also, in Christianity, Islam, and Judaism, the soul's arrival at either heaven or hell is made according to the final Judgment Day that happens at the Reincarnation of the Dead.

When the Roman Catholic Christianity added the doctrine

of **purgatory** in the sixteenth century, the matter became more complex: now souls were given an opportunity to atone for their sins while residing in a kind of interim area between heaven and hell.

While Many Christians, Jews, and Muslims believe that the dead will lie asleep in their graves until the Last Judgment, others in those same faiths maintain that judgment is pronounced immediately after death. Likewise, the concept of the "World to Come" in Jewish writings may refer to heaven or foretell of a future redemption on Earth.

All the major faiths believe that after the soul has left the body, it moves on to another existence. Some faiths contend that the soul ascends to paradise or descends into hell. Others believe that it may achieve a rebirth into another physical body or may merge with the Divine in eternal unity. Traditional Christianity, Islam, and Judaism envision a resurrection of a physical body at a time of final judgment, but the soul is of greater value and purpose than its physical body. The material, physical shell within which Humans dwell during their lifetime, is nothing more than clay or ashes into which God had breathed the breath of life. The physical body is a temporary possession that a Human **has**, not what a person **is**.

How do Buddhism and Hinduism View the Afterlife

Buddhism was established by Buddha - the founder/prophet of Buddhism (circa 567–487 B.C.E.). It perceives that the spiritual essence, the divine part of a living being, the **Atman**, is eternal and seeks to unite with the Universal Soul, the **Brahman**.

Buddhism and Hinduism emerged in Southeast Asia. Buddhism teaches that an individual is but a transient combination of five aggregates (**skandhas**) - matter, sensation, perception, predisposition, and consciousness, and has no permanent soul. Of all the major world religions, only Buddhism does not perceive an eternal metaphysical aspect of the Human personality, the soul, in the same way that the other religions do.

Hinduism (no known founder) is an aggregate of religions exemplified by the term **Dharma**. Dharma can be translated from Sanskrit as "truth, justice and honest living."

According to many world religions, when an individual dies the soul is judged or evaluated, and then is sent to what is perceived as its eternal place - heaven or hell.

A Hindu or Buddhist expects to encounter **YAMA**, the god of the dead. In the Hindu scriptures, YAMA holds dominion over the "bright realms" and can be influenced by "bribe"-offerings of the souls' relatives and friends which are intended to mitigate their punishment.

In the Buddhist tradition, YAMA is the lord of hell, who administers punishment according to everyone's karma (the cause and effect of his or her actions on Earth). In both variations of religion, YAMA is comparable to **Satan,** Whereas in Christian belief, Satan is both the creator of evil and the accuser of Human sins.

Both Buddhism and Hinduism place YAMA, God of the dead, in the position of a judge in the afterlife. The following

15

passages from the "Rig-Veda" depict the special reverence with which YAMA was held. In India's religious classic work, the "Bhagavad Gita" ("Song of the Lord"), the nature of the soul is defined: "It is born not, nor does it ever die, nor shall it die, after having been brought to life"…

While the Buddhist texts recognize the existence of a self as a being that distinguishes one person from another, the Buddhist teachings also state that the Christian, Hindu, Jewish, and Muslim concepts of an eternal metaphysical soul is inaccurate. To a Buddhist, the Human person is but a temporary assemblage of five elements, both physical and psychical, and none of these five individual elements can be identified as the "essential self", nor can the sum of them constitute the "essential self."

Because a Human is composed of elements that are always in a state of flux, always dissolving and combining with each other in new ways, it is impossible to suggest that an individual could retain the same "soul-self" for eternity. The Buddhist doctrine, therefore, talks about an **"anatman", (no-self)**.

Although Buddha denied the Hindu concept of an immortal self that passes through a series of incarnations, he did accept the doctrines of **"karma** and **"samsara"** (rebirth).

If Buddha recognized rebirth into another lifetime, but did not believe in an essential self or soul then what would be reborn? The Buddhist answer is difficult to comprehend: the various components are in a perpetual process of change that constitutes Human beings. They do not reassemble themselves by random chance. Karmic laws determine the nature of a person's rebirth. Various aspects which make up a functioning Human during his or her lifetime enter the **Santana**, the **"chain of being,"** whose various links are related by the law of cause and effect. While there is no Atman, for an individual self that cannot be reincarnated, there is a **"contingent self"** that exists from moment to moment.

This self is comprised of aggregates that are burdened with the consequences of previous actions and bear the potential to be reborn again and again. Because the aggregates of each living person bear within them the fruits of past actions and desires, death sets in motion an immediate retribution for the consequences of these deeds: the person must be reborn again into the unceasing cycle of **karma** and **samsara**. However, **dharma**, the physical and moral laws that govern the universe, flow through everything and everyone, thereby continually changing and rearranging every aspect of the Human. Although driven by **karma**, the **dharma** rearranges the process of rebirth to form a new individual.

In his first sermon, the "**Noble Truth of Suffering (Duka)**", Buddha presented his views on the aggregates that constitute the Human condition: "the Noble Truth of Suffering" is this: "Birth is suffering, sorrow and lamentation, pain, grief, and despair. Association with the unpleasant is suffering, dissociation from the pleasant is suffering. Not to get what one wants is suffering. In brief, the five aggregates of attachment are suffering.

In the "**Dhammapada** (147:51) Buddha speaks further of the destiny of all Human flesh in graphic terms: "Behold this beautiful body, a mass of sores, a heaped-up lump, diseased, nothing lasts, nothing persists, thoroughly worn out is this body, a nest of diseases, perishable. Truly, life ends in death....of bones is this house made, plastered with flesh and blood. Herein are stored decay, death, conceit, and hypocrisy. Even ornamented royal chariots wear out. So too the body reaches old age. But the **Dharma** of the **Good** does not grow old. Thus is the Good revealed".

Buddha's advice to all those who wish to rise above the karmic laws of death and rebirth is to live a contemplative, religious life: "Men who have not led a religious life and have not laid up "treasure" in their youth - perish like old herons in a lake without fish. Men who have laid up a treasure. lie like worn-out bow, sighing after the past". (Dhammapada 155:56)

Dharma is the path to **nirvana,** which can represent the final extinction of the desire to exist. It can also suggest a high level of mystical experience achieved through deep meditation or trance. It never means the complete annihilation of the self but only the squelching of the wish to be reborn. Most often, nirvana is meant to indicate a transformed state of Human consciousness which achieves a reality independent of the material world.

Once the desire to continue existence in a material flesh-form has been extinguished and "when a son of Buddha fulfils his course in the world to come, he becomes Buddha." To achieve Buddhahood is comparable to realizing Brahma, the Absolute and Ultimate. Once these levels have been attained, it is believed that one is freed forever from material reality and becomes one with eternal reality.

There are many schools of historical **Buddhism—Hinayana, Mahayana, Tantric, and Pure Land**-and it is difficult to find consensus among them concerning the afterlife. The Tibetan Buddhism's "**Book of the dead"** provides an important source for an understanding of the Buddhist concept of the afterlife's journey of the soul: A **lama** (priest) sits at the side of the deceased and recites a text from the "Book of the Dead". The text recited is - "a state of being aware of something within oneself" – this is a ritual which is thought to revive the life force within the body." It gives the deceased the power to embark upon a 49-day journey through the intermediate stage between death and rebirth. Such a recitation by the lama might include the following words from the "Book of the Dead": "Since you no longer have a material body of flesh and blood, whatever may come - sounds, lights, or rays - all three, are unable to harm you. You are incapable of dying. It is quite sufficient for you to know that these three apparitions are your own thought-forms. Recognize this to reach **"bardo"** (the intermediate state after death).

The passage of the soul from this world to the next, is described in the **Brihadarankyaka Upanishad**: The Self, having enjoyed in dreams the pleasures of sense, goes hither and thither. It experienced good and evil and hastens back to the state of waking from which he had started. As a man passes from dream to wakefulness, so does he pass from this life to the next. Then the point of his heart, where the nerves join, is lighted by the "Light of the Self". By this light he departs either through the eye, or through the gate of the skull, or through some other aperture of the body... The Self remains conscious and as conscious, the dying man goes to his abode. The deeds of this life, and the impressions he left behind, follow him - as a caterpillar that reached the end of a blade of grass takes hold of another blade and draws itself to it, so the self, having left behind it a body unconscious, takes hold of another body and draws himself to it.

By the third century B.C.E. Hinduism had adopted a cyclical world view of lives and rebirths in which the earlier concepts of heaven and hell, an afterlife system of reward and punishment, were replaced by intermediate states between lifetimes. Hindu cosmology depicted three **Lokas**, (realms) - heaven, Earth, and the netherworld. In addition, there are fourteen levels in which varying degrees of suffering or bliss await the soul between physical existences. Seven of these heavens or hells rise above Earth and seven descend below. According to the great Hindu teacher Sankara of the ninth century and the school of **Advaita Vedanta**, the eventual goal of the soul's odyssey is **moxa**, a complete liberation from samsara, (death and rebirth) This would lead to **nirvana** - the ultimate union of **atman** with the divine **Brahma.** In the eleventh century, Ramanuja and the school of

Visitadvaita saw the bliss of nirvana as a complete oneness of the soul with God.

In the last centuries before our time, a form of Hinduism known as **bhakti** spread rapidly across India. Bhakti envisions a loving relationship between God and the devout believer that is based upon grace. Those devotees who had prepared themselves by a loving attitude, a study of the scriptures, and devotion to **Lord Krishna**, may free themselves from an endless cycle of death and rebirth. Eternal life is granted to devotees who at the time of death, give up their physical body with only thoughts of Lord Krishna on their minds. (Lord Krishna is a major deity in Hinduism. He is the god of protection, compassion, softness and love).

Author's note: I have brought a lot of material about Buddhism and Hinduism, since they are among the largest religions in the world, and deal very considerably with what happens to persons' Physical bodies and souls, before and after death.

How does Islam View the Afterlife

Muhammad, the founder/prophet of Islam, (570 c.e.–632 c.e.), appears to have regarded the soul as the essential self of a Human being. But adhering to the ancient Judeo-Christian tradition he also considered the physical body as a requirement for life after death. The word for the independent soul is **Nafs**, similar in meaning to the Greek **psyche**. The word for the aspect of the soul that gives Humans their dignity and elevates them above the animals is **Ruh**, equivalent to the Greek **nous.** These two aspects of the soul combine the lower and the higher, the Human and the divine.

About the concept of a soul, Islam envisions a Human as a being of spirit and body. The creation of Adam as described in the **Qur'an** (the holy Muslim book) is reminiscent of **Genesis** in the Jewish Bible. Muhammad was in contact with Jewish merchants in the Arab desert, and the Qur'an was written under their influence by literate Arabs:

"The Lord announces to the angels that he is going to create a man of clay and that he will breathe his spirit into him after he has given him form". And He originated the creation of man out of clay, then He fashioned his progeny with an extraction of "mean water" (matter closest to Godliness) then He shaped him and breathed His spirit in him." (Qur'an 32:8–9)

As in the other major religions, how one lives on Earth, will prepare the soul for the afterlife and there are promises of a paradise or the warnings of a place of torment. The Qur'an (57:20) contains an admonition concerning the transient nature of life on Earth and a reminder of the two possible destinations that await the soul after death: "Know you that the present life is but a sport and a diversion, an adornment and a cause of boasting among you and a rivalry in wealth and children. It is like a rain whose vegetation pleases the unbelievers; then it withers, and you see it turning yellow, then it becomes straw. And in the Hereafter, there is grievous punishment, and forgiveness from God and good pleasure whereas the present life is but the joy of delusion."

Muhammad speaks of the Last Judgment after which there will be a resurrection of the dead which will bring everlasting bliss to the righteous and hellish torments to the wicked. The judgment will be individual. No soul will be able to help a friend or family member, he warns. No soul will be able to give satisfaction or intercede for another.

While the doctrine of the resurrection of the body has never been abandoned in Islam, later students of the Qur'an, sought to define the soul in more metaphysical terms and a belief in the pre-existence of souls was established. In this view, Allah (the Muslim God) kept a treasure-house of souls in paradise available for their respective incarnations on Earth.

The Islamic paradise is in many ways an extension of the legendary Garden of Eden in the Bible. It is a beautiful place filled with trees, flowers, and fruit, but it really cannot be described in Human terms. It is far more wonderful than any person could ever imagine. "All who obey God, and the Apostle (Muhammad), are in the group of those on whom is the grace of God: The Prophets who teach, the sincere lovers of Truth, the witnesses (martyrs) who testify, and the righteous who do good: Ah! What a beautiful fellowship!" (Qur'an 4:69). The Muslim paradise also contains beautiful virgins (in flocks of 72). They are given to soldiers who fought and died for Allah.

How does Christianity View the Afterlife

Note: Most probably, a lot of my readers (if I shall have any at all...) may be Christians. Therefore, please modify the following statements according to your own knowledge).

The core of the Christian faith is the belief in the resurrection of Jesus (6 b.c.e.–c. 30 c.e.) after his death on the cross, and the promise of life everlasting to all who accept his divinity.

Because Christianity rose out of Judaism, the teachings of Jesus as recorded in the gospels, reflect many of the Jewish beliefs of the soul and the afterlife. Primarily: that a reunion of body and soul will be accomplished in the next world.

The accounts of the appearance of Jesus to his apostles after his resurrection show how completely they believed that they beheld him in the flesh even to the extreme of the skeptical Thomas who inserted his fingertips into the still-open wounds of the crucifixion to see if Jesus is in there or resurrected. Jesus told them: "A spirit does not have flesh and bones as you see that I have." Then, to prove still further his "physicality he asks if they have anything for him to eat."

Paul (?–c. 68 c.e.), the apostle (and once avid persecutor of Christians), may have received his revelation from the voice of Jesus within a blinding light while he was traveling on the road to Damascus... When he preached in Athens, he discovered that it would be a challenge to convince others to believe in the physical resurrection of the dead. The assembled Athenians listened politely to his message of a new faith but then mocked him and walked away when he began to speak of dead bodies standing up and being reborn. To these cultured men and women who had been exposed to Plato's philosophy that the material body was but a fleshly prison from which the soul was freed by death, the very notion of resurrecting decaying bodies was repugnant.

Paul refused to acknowledge defeat. Because he had been educated as a Greek, he set about achieving a compromise between the "resurrection theology" that is being taught by his fellow apostles, and the "Platonic view of the soul", so widely accepted in Greek society. Paul knew that Plato had viewed the soul as composed of three constituents: the **nous** (the rational soul) is immortal and incarnated in a physical body; the **Thumos** (passion, heart, spirit); and **epithumetikos** (desire). Therefore, he decided to incorporate them in his preachings. After many hardships, imprisonments, and public humiliations, Paul worked out a theology that envisioned Human nature as composed of three essential elements: the physical body, the psyche and the life-principle, much like the Hebrew concept of the **nephesh,** and the **pneuma**, the spirit, the inner self. Developing his thought further, he made the distinction between the "**natural body**" of a living person that dies and is buried, and the "**spiritual body,**" which is resurrected.

In 1 Corinthians 15:35–44, Paul writes: "but some will ask, "How are the dead raised? With what kind of body do they come? - You foolish men! What you sow does not come to life unless it dies, and what you sow is not the body, which is to be, but a bare kernel... God gives it a body as He has chosen and to each kind of seed its own body. For not all flesh is alike... There are celestial bodies and there are terrestrial bodies; but the glory of the celestial is one, and the glory of the terrestrial is another... So, it is with the resurrection of the dead. What is sown is perishable, what is raised is imperishable. If it is sown in dishonor; it is raised in glory. If it is sown in weakness, it is raised in power. If it is sown in the physical body, it is raised in a spiritual body. If there is a physical body, there is also a spiritual body."

Paul had begun to mix Platonic and Jewish philosophies in a manner that would be acceptable to thousands of new converts to Christianity. Still, he could not free himself completely from the Hebrew tradition that insisted upon some bodily form in the afterlife. However inconsistent it might appear to some students of theology, Paul and his fellow first-century Christian missionaries taught that while the immortal soul within was the most essential aspect of a person's existence, in order for a proper afterlife, one day there would be a judgment and the righteous would be rewarded with reconstituted bodies.

The early church fathers began more and more to shape Christian doctrines that reflected Plato's metaphysical philosophy, but they remained greatly divided over the particular nature of the immortal soul. The Platonists saw the soul as supra-individual and remaining within the universal cosmic soul after its final ascent to oneness with the Divine. The Christian philosophers could not be shaken from their position that God created each soul to be immortal and individual, irrevocably connected to the afterlife. Among them was Tertullian (Circa160 c.e.–220 c.e.) who defined the soul as having sprung directly from the breath of God, thereby making it immortal. The body, in the Platonic view, was merely the instrument of the **anima** - the soul. The highly respected Alexandrian scholar Origen (circa 185 c.e.–254 c.e.) theorized that in the beginning, God had created a certain number of spirit- entities who received physical bodies or spiritual bodies, as determined by their respective merits. Some might be appointed Human forms, while others, according to their conduct, would be elevated to angelic status, or relegated to the position of demons.

Such a concept of the pre-existence of souls, seemed too close to reincarnation for those learned Christian scholars that assembled for the First Council of Constantinople in 543. By then, the church doctrine had decreed that it was given to each soul to live once, to die, and then to await the Day of Judgement when Christ will return to Earth. Despite his prestige as a learned and wise church father, Origen's views were condemned as heretical.

The prevailing view of the early Christian church was the one espoused by Jerome (342 c.e.–420 c.e.). He envisioned God as creating new souls as they were required for the new bodies born to Human parents on Earth. Orthodox contemporary Christianity continued to maintain the position that each newborn person receives a new soul that has never existed in any other form.

In Christian doctrine, the soul is superior to the body because of its divine origin, and because it is immortal. But the belief in a resurrection of the physical body is also an essential aspect of both the Apostles' Creed and the Nicene Creed. They declared that after the Last Judgment, Jesus shall once again appear to "judge the living and the dead."

In Chapter 25 of Matthew, Jesus tells a parable of how the "Son of Man" is to come and sit on his throne. There, the people of all nations will gather before him so that he might separate them as a shepherd separates the sheep from the goats. Those individuals who loved their neighbors as themselves, will be rewarded with eternal life. But those who have chosen greed and self-interest will be sent away into eternal punishment. In Acts 17:31 it is stated that God has appointed Jesus Christ to judge the world; Acts 10:42 again names Christ as the one "ordained by God to be the judge of the living and the dead."

The early Christian Church believed that the Second Coming of Jesus is imminent, and that many who were alive in the time of the apostles, would live to see his return in the clouds. When this remarkable event shall occur, it would signal the end of time in which Jesus Christ would raise the dead and judge those who would ascend to heaven, and those who would suffer the everlasting torments of hell. The delay in the "Second Coming," forced the Church to adjust its theology to acknowledge that the time of judgment for everyone would arrive at the time of the person's death.

For the traditional Christian, heaven is the everlasting dwelling place of God and angelic beings who have served him faithfully since the beginning. There, those Christians who had been redeemed through faith in Jesus as the Christ, will be with him forever in glory. Liberal Christians acknowledge that as Jesus promised, there are many mansions in his father's kingdom, where those of other faiths may also dwell. For more fundamental and conservative Christians, the terrifying graphic images depicted over the centuries of the Last Judgment, have been too powerful to be eliminated from doctrinal teachings. So, they envision a beautiful place high above the Earth, where only true believers in Jesus may reign with him.

Hell, in traditional Christian thought is a place of eternal torment for those who have been damned after the Last Judgment. It is pictured as a barren pit filled with flames - the images developed out of the Hebrew **Sheol** and the Greek **Hades,** as the final resting places for the damned dead.

Roman Catholic Christianity continues to depict hell as a state of unending punishment for the unrepentant but over five centuries ago, the councils of Florence (1439) and Trent (1545–63), defined the concept of **purgatory:** an intermediate state after death, during which the souls have opportunities to expiate certain of their sins. Devoted family members can offer prayers and oblations which can assist those souls in purgatory to atone for their earthly transgressions and achieve a restoration of their union with God.

Protestant Christianity does not offer its followers the opportunities for afterlife redemption afforded by purgatory, or any other intermediate spiritual state. But it has removed much of the fear of hell and replaced it with an emphasis upon grace and faith. While fundamentalist Protestants retain the traditional views of heaven and hell, there are many contemporary Protestant clergy who have rejected the idea of a place of eternal torment for condemned souls as incompatible with the belief in a loving God of forgiveness. Hell has been transformed from a place of everlasting suffering to an afterlife state of being without the presence of God. For liberal Christian theologians, the entire teaching of a place of everlasting damnation has been completely rejected in favor of the love of Jesus for all Humanity.

How does Judaism View the Afterlife

In Judaism, when the God formed man out of the dust of the ground and breathed into his nostrils the breath of life, then man became a living being" (Genesis 2:7). In the second chapter of Genesis, it is again repeated that **Yahweh**, (the god of Israel) breathed his breath into the "dust man", on reincarnation. Interestingly, Yahweh also bestowed the breath of life into the animals that flourished in the Garden of Eden, and they, too, are living souls. **Nephesh,** the soul, is closely associated with blood - the life-substance which is drained at death from the body. Thus, the Hebrew tradition established the recognition that a living person is a composite entity made up of flesh and nephesh, the spiritual essence. "The body is the sheath of the soul," states the Talmud (the Jewish law book) in Sanhedrin 108a.

The early Hebrews believed that after death, the soul descended to Sheol, a place deep inside the Earth. In Sheol, the spirits of the dead were consigned to dust and gloom. "All go unto one place; all are of the dust and all turn to dust again" (Ecclesiastes 3:20).

By the time the Book of Daniel was written in about 165 b.c.e., the belief had been established that the dead would be resurrected and receive judgment: "Many of those who lie dead in the ground, will rise from death. Some of them will be given eternal life, and others will receive nothing but eternal shame and disgrace. Everyone who has been wise, will shine bright as the sky above, and everyone who has led others to please God, will shine like the stars" (Daniel 12: 2 - 4).

While the verses from Daniel are the only ones in Jewish scripture that specifically mention the afterlife of the soul, the subject is widely discussed in the Rabbinic literature, in the **Kabbalah**, and in Jewish folklore. The soul is believed to have its roots in the world of the divine, and after the physical death of the body, the soul returns to the place of its spiritual origin. Some Jewish thinkers refer to the soul's sojourn on Earth as a kind of exile to be served, until its reunion with God.

By the second century B.C.E., many Jewish teachers had been exposed to the Greek concept of the soul as the essential self that exists prior to the earthly body, into which it is born, and which survives the body's physical death. However, the old traditions retained the view that an existence in the afterlife requires the restoration of **the whole person.**

As Jewish thinking on the afterlife progressed from earlier beliefs, a school of thought arose maintaining that at the arrival of the Messiah, God would raise the dead to life again. Then he will pass judgment upon them -rewarding the righteous and punishing the wicked. Such a resurrection was viewed as a restoration of persons who would possess both physical bodies and spirits. Thus, the traditional philosophy that to be a living person was to be a psycho-physical unit and not an eternal soul temporarily inhabiting a mortal body, was reinforced. More often, however, the references to a judgment of the dead in Judaism recall the scene in the seventh chapter of the Book of Daniel: The "Ancient of Days" opens the books of life and passes judgment on the whole kingdoms of the Earth, rather than on individuals.

According to some circles of Jewish thought, in the actual Day of Judgment, the **Yom HaDin**, the resurrection of the dead will occur when the Messiah comes. On that fateful day, both Israel and the Gentile nations will be summoned to the place of judgment by the blowing of the great **shofar** (ram's horn), to awaken the people from their spiritual slumber. The prophet Elijah will return and set about the task of reconciling families who have become estranged. The day when the Lord judges, "will be dark, very dark, without a ray of light" (Amos 5:20). Those who have maintained righteous lives and kept their covenant with God, will be taken to the heavenly paradise. Those who have been judged as deserving of punishment for their misdeeds, will be sent to **Gehinnom (hell),** to stay there for a length of time commensurate with the seriousness of their transgressions.

The Jewish religion is unique in stating that life on earth is full of suffering. This was indeed the case of the terrible holocaust and the deportations by the Babylonian and the Assyrian kings, from which they returned to their homeland just recently. During their dispersal in many countries of the world, the Jews suffered pogroms and oppression. No wonder then that the Jewish Talmud tried to console the sufferers that "the more grief in life, the greater will be their reward in the afterlife". Unfortunately, suffering through life is not the lot of just Jews, but of too many people all over the world!

When dealing with life after death, what are the similarities between religions

Eternal life: Occurs in either heaven or hell, depending on the individual.

The Essence of Afterlife Beliefs: While the world's religions offer diverse perspectives on life after death, fundamental similarities endure. The notion of reward or punishment based on earthly conduct is a recurring theme.

Sacred texts: Teachings in scriptures or traditions of Christianity, Judaism, and Islam promise an afterlife.

🍎 Continued existence in some form after physiological death: The belief that some aspect of an individual survives after death. Usually, the individual's soul is common to the great majority of the world's religions.

🍎 Beliefs on life after death for most religious people are about fairness and justice. Whether karma decides the next life. or God sends a soul to a place of reward or punishment, most religions teach that everyone will face consequences for how they have lived, and no one will escape justice in the afterlife.

🍎 Beyond the major world religions, myriad other beliefs shape Humanity's understanding of the afterlife: Indigenous cultures exhibit a kaleidoscope of beliefs, ranging from ancestral spirits to reincarnation. Ancient civilizations like Egypt, wove intricate narratives of the afterlife, envisioning a profound journey into the unknown.

🍎 The creation of Adam as described in the Qur'an, is reminiscent of Genesis in the Judeo-Christian Bible: The Lord announces to the angels that he is going to create a Human of clay and that he will breathe his spirit into him, after he has given him form. "And He originated the creation of man out of clay, then He fashioned his progeny of an extraction of mean water, then He shaped him and breathed His spirit in him." (Qur'an 32:8–9)

A NOTE FROM THE AUTHOR:

THERE IS A GENERAL AGREEMENT AMONG VARIOUS PEOPLE THAT RELIGIONS RESTRAIN THEIR ADHERENTS FROM GROSS VIOLENCE AND MURDER.

I BELIEVE THAT THIS IS **UNTRUE:** MUSLIMS HATE JEWS AND CHRISTIANS AND THEY PROSECUTE THEM, JUST BECAUSE THEY WORSHIP OTHER GODS.

JEWS HATE MUSLIMS BECAUSE THEY KILL JEWS AND PARTICULARLY ISRAELIS. THEY HATED CHRISTIANS BECAUSE THEY KILLED JEWS IN THE PAST.

CHRISTIANS MAY ABHOR MUSLIMS FOR THE SAME REASON – THEY KILED CHRISTIANS.

IN THE PAST, VARIOUS CHRISTIAN SECTS MADE TERRIBLE WARS ON EACH OTHER.

THEREFORE, I WANT TO STRESS THAT I BELIEVE THAT RELIGIONS ARE THE ROOT OF ALL OR MOST EVIL. THEY FOSTER RACIAL DISCRIMINATION AND MANY WARS IN OUR WORLD. MOST PEOPLE WILL SAY THAT I AM EXAGGERATING SOMEWHAT. BUT I STAND BY MY POSITION!!!

BOOK 4

A complete- length science fiction novel on Reincarnation.

"THE REINCARNATION"

"QUO VADIS DOMINE"
(Where shall we go, Oh Leader?)

The main protagonist of the story said: "My friends call me "moose". This moniker had stuck to me in high school. At that time, playing football, I was a running back who held the football protected in my left hand and used my right hand to knock aside forcibly the defending opposite players. Therefore, I reminded all the spectators and the players of a moose: both because of my bulk and height, and because my hand thrusted the opposing players aside, just like the horn of a moose would thrust. Like a moose, I was six feet tall (tall for my age) and weighed 200 pounds. I had a brown-blackish hair like a moose's fur color, brown eyes and a large, curved nose...

These extraordinary attributes made me feel like a giant among pygmies (my teammates or the opposing team) and as a leader among the men. My real name was Moses Daniel Frank, and I was Jewish.

Unfortunately, my prowess could not avert a killer: I contracted a Sarcoma tumor in my right leg and eventually, after amputations in both my legs, I perished painfully. My bereaved family gave me a traditional Jewish funeral and my mourning mother visited my grave at least once a week for a whole year.

Before I died, I assumed that I was going to rest in my grave till my whole body will rot and turn to ashes. Therefore, imagine my surprise when I became conscious, and a transparent ghost rose out of my entombed body. My ghost even penetrated through the marble plate over my body (this is a part of the Jewish funeral rites – a plate of marble is placed over the body of the deceased). Then my transparent ghost started to fly to some unknown destination and my ghostly flight ended at the entrance of a dark tunnel. I entered the tunnel and at its end I found myself in a brightly lit cavern. The cavern contained many confused ghosts like me running aimlessly to-and-fro, or just sitting apathetically.

Among these ghosts, I identified three of my long-dead relatives: my grandfather, my grandmother and a younger aunt. All three wanted to embrace me all-at-once. I ended by hugging all three together. Even as a ghost, (I immediately understood that I was one), my bulk was still very large...

I asked my aunt, the smartest of my three relatives, what was happening. Unfortunately, she did not know about his family. I realized that I must rely on myself to find out what is happening, and my brain started to sift through its grey matter. One insistent memory started to crystalize clearly among others: My rabbi, (Jewish ordained religious functionary), recited once during my Bar-Mitzva studies an interesting tradition: (Bar-Mitzva is the Jewish feast to celebrate, at 13 years, the maturation of a Jewish boy) "when the Messiah will come, all dead Jews will reincarnate and roll through long subterranean tunnels to Palestine, the land of our ancestors". At that time, I filed this statement in some "drawer" of my brain and now I "freed" it. It made me realize that all of us in the cavern were reincarnated and did not know what to do with this wonderful gift.

Then I dimly remembered that during my life on earth, I was a leader in my football team. Therefore, I decided to assert myself here, in the cavern, and to try to help these confused, reincarnated ghosts and reincarnated ghost- children (there were also a few children in the cavern…)!

I raised myself to the whole stature of the six feet of my hazy specter and cried: "Hi there dear people! Hi there dear children! Please listen to me! My name is Moses. As most of you may know, Moses was the prophet who led the People of Israel through the Sinai desert, from Egypt to Palestine. In Palestine, another prophet, whose name was Joshua, carved for the Israelis a new-old state! "old", because it was once the land of their ancestors.

I would like to act for you as your "prophet" and lead you to a new home. Please let us vote: does everybody concur to accept me as your leader?" all the confused ghosts concurred (I did not expect anything less…). "Great!" I said. "I shall take all of you from this dismal cavern to a new abode!"

"Listen to me, dear people! Now we are all ghosts! But I ask you to gird your loins and establish from the lot of us a **new nation**. A nation made of **past** Christians, **past** Muslims, **past** Hindus and **past** Jews! Please relegate all your old identities to the past and acquire a new identity as **a nation of reincarnateds**.!"

I continued: "When I said that I shall lead you to a new abode, I did not mean to our old earth! it is already crowded, and I think that the "God" or "Gods" who reincarnated us, do not want the "Earthiest" to learn about reincarnation. Let the "earthiest" wait until their own turn comes to reincarnate– their own death - HA, HA. HA!"

"As your leader. I think that I shall lead you to **a new** planet **in the wide space**, although I must admit, I do not know yet how to do it!"

'This reincarnation "business" is very new to you, as it is for me. But, as your leader, I have already given it some thought. I think that it is a great gift! many of you, though not all, suffered through life, and even died miserably in wars! I do not know for sure who sent us this gift, but it can only be our respective gods. Let us avail ourselves of this gift and LIVE AGAIN!"

Dear citizens of our new nation. I had called the extremely potent beings who reincarnated us and removed us from our graves, as "god" or "gods", because I do not know who else they can be. Since we need to refer to them, let us call them as "God(s)" for the time being.

Recently, before I abandoned my soul to my maker, I read a thought-provoking book called *"Many lives, many masters,"* written by Dr. Brian L. Weiss. Dr Weiss is a psychiatrist, and as a traditional psychotherapist he treated one of his patients, a beautiful 30-year-old woman called Cathrin, with conventional psychotherapy, but could not cure her. She suffered from unexplained terrors and nightmares and did not talk throughout all the psychotherapy sessions. He decided, finally, to treat her under hypnosis. He was extremely surprised when, under the hypnosis, the reticent Cathryn began talking and recalled all her past life traumas. They held the key to her recurring nightmares and anxiety attacks, and she recovered swiftly.

However, when she was under hypnosis, she also began to "channel" messages from some unknown sources - highly developed spiritual entities - whom she called "masters". These messages contained remarkable revelations about Doctor Weiss' own family and his dead son, although before the hypnosis she knew nothing about. Using hypnosis, he embarked on a new, meaningful phase of his own career. Dr. Weiss thought that these "Masters" represented or were connected to what Carl Yung (a great psychiatrist and psychotherapist), called "a collective sub-consciousness" - the source of the energy that surrounds us and contains the sum of all our memories.

I do not believe in God. Therefore, <u>FOR ME,</u> as a working hypothesis, I shall adopt the potent, powerful "masters" of Cathrin as those who delivered to us the gift of this reincarnation "marvel". However, I realize that most of you believe in God, especially after our reincarnation. For your sake, I shall name the Masters as "Deities". Any objections? Please raise your hand!" After some thinking, only a few people objected…"So," I said: "The ayes for "Deities" have it! Therefore "Deities" they are from now on! If indeed. they are those who reincarnated us, I hope that they may send us in the future many more "marvels" like the reincarnation!"

I must add that most of my group did not comprehend Dr. Weiss' story that I brought. It was enough for them to enjoy the reincarnation marvel and to live again. However, I could see that some of the more intelligent ghosts were very impressed by my story.

"Solidification" and the advent of the Miraculous "cells"

After the naming of our benefactors, I continued: "Here is what my "genius" brain suggested to me: Ha, Ha, Ha...we need to shed our "ghostly" attire, because the job that awaits us in our future home-planet will require hard work. Therefore, we must acquire solid substance and form, and muscles too! How to do it, I do not know yet. But I am sure that our Deities would want us to "solidify". Perhaps some form of meditation, or "Deep prayer", shall do it? If not - let us all go to sleep. My aunt, who was one of the first ladies in this cavern, told me that all of you could not sleep because of your apparent worry and confusion. Now that you are calmer, I hope, let us try our best to sleep in order achieve "solidification?"

I finished my discourse and decided to be the first one to meditate... I sat in a lotus position (being a flexible ghost helped), and I sank into meditation. I needed to meditate for only about five minutes, and "HOP", I easily solidified!

My whole group imitated me or at least sat quietly, trying to meditate.

In a few minutes I was gratified to see that my first suggestion as a leader, worked well – one by one they "solidified." All around the cavern I heard happy cries of people who were glad to get rid of their "ghostliness". Being ghosts reminded them too much of their lives and deaths. All of them, including the women, wore overalls made of some metallic fabric that looked very durable and, perhaps, will withstand the rigors of building in our new planet. Deities willing...

I watched the process of solidification all around me and was totally surprised to see that they lacked what I would call a "1:1" process. Some big males solidified into short women. Some delicate women solidified into muscular males. Near me, a large "ox" of a man turned into a small boy. What impressed me most was that all the solidified men and women exhibited hard, swollen

39

muscles that they happily felt. I was completely unprepared for the trans-gendering and the uneven size-transformations. I tried to hide my amusement until I saw that I was not alone. A great hilarity reigned in the cavern! The former confused and depressed people were rejuvenated! I thought that the great changes that happened to my group, came as a result of their former lives: If they lad an honest life and helped their fellow men and women they stayed large and even taller than before. If they were self-centered and even evil - they turned into small children.

I raised my voice again and told the whole group not to fear, and to enjoy their physical changes. I went even as far as to say that the new women-to-men trans-gendering occurred because some women envied men all their life and wanted to be males, and vice versa for men who turned into beautiful, muscular, women…

The solidified people tried to feel their backs for wings but could not find any. This was an unexpected finding! How can a reincarnated, solidified, person reach a suitable destination in space, if not by flying?

However, looking around them, they saw that each one of them found themselves inside a big square Perspex "cell", that they could not understand its purpose. Each cell had a toilet and a robot-like machine that contained a computer and a computer screen. The six walls of the cubic cells were extremely well-welded and looked contiguous. We found that we could freely breathe in the cells, because each cell contained air, and some small boxes filled with black powder.

Later found that the powder is "activated charcoal". This material is known to absorb the waste-product of Carbon dioxide that people exhale. Later I also learned that the robot-computer continually poured Oxygen into the cells.

Locked in my cell, I was unhappy to notice that I cannot communicate with my people even by shouting. My group numbered a very large number of cells which were dispersed along a very large area. I cursed profusely, but then my aunt, who self-nominated herself as my deputy (I concurred…) and was in the cell closest to mine, heard me cursing and said: "Moose, I think I know why you are cursing!. Look at your computer screen. Do not worry about a lack of communication with your group! You "star" in all the group's screens. The robot computers are like television, and all our people even heard your curses…"

I Immediately realized that since I could communicate with all my group and be seen by all of them, I need to establish rules and timetables for those who wish to talk to the leader. I also realized that when I must obey a call of nature during talking hours, to stand in such a way that will not exhibit my private parts…

In the wake of my success with the solidification I decided to test the capabilities of my computer. I said to my group: "I am going to experiment with my robot-like computer. I am sure that no frightful monster will jump from it. Until now, our "Deities" never disappointed us and never damaged us." While saying that, I pressed the "ENTER" key…

No monster materialized, but a writing appeared on the screen - "Hello Moses! Would you like a beverage or food?" I was completely flabbergasted because how can a robot know my real name? and in addition, also to supply me with a beverage or with food? On earth, all of us were familiar with vending machines that were filled with new supplies every night. But here, behind the computer, there was no room for an attendant or a maintenance person or boxes of new supplies… Also, how did the robot know my name? But then, I realized that as the leader of our group, the computer stored my picture and the pictures and the names of all the people in my group. As for the beverages and the food, after all, our Deities were omnipotent, weren't they?

Smiling, I answered the robot politely: "Hi Robo, I shall call you Robo, if you do not mind. I want a cup of tea, please. hot, and with two teaspoons of sugar". Immediately a photograph of a cup with tea appeared on the screen and the screen opened and allowed me to pick up the cup. I tasted the tea, and it was "heavenly" - some sort of a Chinese blend.

Immediately all the members of my group started to experiment, but I immediately cautioned them to ask only for liquid foods. Liquid foods can be easily discarded into the toilet, which was our only disposal chute to the outside, while hard food will clog it. However, some daring spirits asked their computers for solid food like chicken or steak, caused stoppages and cried to me for help. I told them to meditate and ask the Deities for machines that would suck out the clogging solid food. The Deities read my mind, and after the daring people got rid of the hard food from the toilets, the Deities left the sucking machines in their cells. as punishment. The Deities only relented after a whole week.

We drank soups and desserts galore, and then I said: "Dear group, till now. We succeeded in everything that we tried. But I worry whether the "leaders-prophets" of other groups in Terra would know how to instruct their ghosts to meditate. to leave their caverns, solidify, etc... (I called "earth" as "Terra" on purpose, to signify that we do not belong to "earth" anymore). I told my group that after we find a suitable planet for us, I shall try to get back somehow to earth and teach the groups how to "solidify", etc. '

When I finished my tirade, I was surprised and gratified to see that my whole group applauded me. My announcement touched their hearts... This is how solidarity should be built within emerging nations!

"Warping" to find a suitable Earth-like planet for habitation

Following the applause that I earned, I said: "I know that you were worried that we do not have wings to fly with. But I hope that we do not need them! I am **an avid Science fiction**

fan, and recently, SF authors started to write about "warping" as a way of an instantaneous travel between stars. "Warping", according to them, is a folding-back, plus removal of large pieces of space, thus achieving instantaneous transit to their intended targets in space. In view of our previous success with meditation, let us try to meditate again to achieve "warping". As before, I shall try it first. If it works, I shall conclude that meditation is a good "**begging**" way to get "**favors**" from our "Deities". I shall try to warp to Phobos, which is one of the moons of Mars. It was a favorite of mine, since it is easy to recognize. I liked to watch it in my city's planetarium.

I meditated for ten minutes very deeply and was elated to see the broken face of Phobos in front of my cell (Phobos was broken, because a long time ago it had been hit by a large meteor). I was sure that all my group was aware of my success since I disappeared, together with my "spacecraft" (my cell)... I warped back and happily informed my group of my success. Despite the success of the warping, I felt a need to warn my group and said: "Dear group, I want to warn you that not every planet will be suitable for our habitation. Some of them will be just gas giants. Most of them may lack a suitable atmosphere for Human breathing. Others may have either freezing or boiling temperature or lack potable water. Only one planet in several thousands may fit for Human habitation. So, our work is cut out for us! Let me say that **now**, as your Prophet, you must admit I never promised an immediate "rose garden"..."

Then I added: "the time had come for us to warp in space and find us a good home-planet. I must admit that in all the time that had recently passed, I dreaded the approach of this action: When I elected myself to be a leader, I "shot my mouth off" and told you that I shall lead you far away from earth - to an earth-like planet". This promise I shall try to fulfill. We shall stay in a galaxy that we know - warp to our Milky Way Galaxy to find us an earth-like planet!.

Planning future warpings

After my promise to find us a suitable home-planet, I lay in bed at night, worried and helpless. I realized that I do not know how to pick a suitable planet for my group.

Finally, in the morning, I hit upon a solution: I shall transfer the problem elsewhere - to people in my group. This is what **councilors** are for, aren't they? – to take a load off the shoulders of their boss/leader. I shall establish a committee of smart people in several areas – in short, councilors! I immediately typed in my computer required A councilor's list, according to what I thought would be required:

1. Two astronomers
2. One atmosphere chemist/air analyst
3. One water specialist/water analyst
4. One heating engineer
5. One refrigeration engineer
6. One forester
7. One Botanist / gardener
8. One wheat farmer

In the morning, I went "on the tube" and told my group that if someone considers himself suitable to be a councilor of the kind in the list that I publicized just now, he ought to apply to Sheindel, my deputy. I also informed my group that every chosen councilor will receive, in the event of successful counselling, important benefits. I transferred the selection process to Sheindel and started to breathe freely again. Since I was very tired because of my busy night, I went calmly to sleep all day.

Sheindel received the names of all applicants and processed them very quickly. Within one week I had an excellent group of experts. Missing was a refrigeration engineer, but I decided that the heating engineer can also oversee refrigeration.

In the first councilors' meeting I told my experts of a motto that I invented: "Terraform and maintain". Then I said: "We shall search for a planet that should be as earth-like as possible. If we cannot find a planet that fits this optimal description, we may need to **Terraform** a sub-optimal planet and **maintain** it for our habitation. To Terraform, obviously, we shall need to change either the atmosphere, the temperature or the ecology of a planet (or even two or all three parameters).

I added: "dear councilors! Today we shall concentrate on the finding of earth-like planets by using our astronomers' expertise. John! You are the senior astronomer with the most experience. Let us hear you first".

John, a tall, fat bespectaled redhead, cleared his throat and said: "Dear Ladies and Gentlemen (there were two of the gentle sex in the committee – the botanist gardener and the forester…). We are in luck! Just three days before I "passed away", there appeared an essay in "Scientific American" on a new earth-like rocky planet (earth is rocky too…). It is called **Kepler 186f**. It is a far-away planet – 493 light years away from earth. The "earthies", as moose called them, shall need very advanced spacecrafts to reach it. But the production of such spacecrafts shall require many more centuries.

Kepler 186f planet circles a red dwarf **star-(Sun)** (not the planet, of course) also called Kepler 186 (but without the 'f'). It has a mass that is 1,76 times that of earth. The Kepler 186 red dwarf **star** has a "habitable zone". A habitable zone is a region around the Center **star** from which the planets can receive a perfect amount of heat. This amount of heat can maintain liquid water on the surface of a planet without freezing or evaporating too quickly. The Kepler 186f **planet** is considered a twin of the Terra. There are also Kepler b, c and d, but they are too hot.

Moose heard John happily and said: "Now, Jordan, it is your turn!" Jordan raised a list of 10 planets on the computer's screen and said: "These planets that I listed in the computer are all **Exoplanets'** (planets that are very far from Terra) and considered to be the most Earth-like alien worlds discovered to date (I specialize in discovering Exoplanets):

1. Gliese-667Cc
2. Kepler-22b
3. Kepler-69c
4. Kepler-62f
5. Kepler-186f ("John's exoplanet")
6. Kepler-442b
7. Kepler-452b
8. Kepler-1649c
9. Proxima Centauri b
10. Trappist-1e

The planets that I listed have two attributes already listed by John for Kepler 186f, they are rocky and are very far from earth. We have the great advantage of "warping" that is provided by our Deities, as Moose already demonstrated to us yesterday. So, let us warp to each one, serially, and find out which will be the most suitable." Moose was overjoyed to hear his two astronomical councilors and decided to start the warp immediately.

Finally warping

Moose asked his two astronomers, Atmosphere analyzer (Bill) and the water specialist (Clark)t to form a small search committee to warp and search with him. The four comrades, other than Moose, were two couples where each couple resembled Laurel and Hardy. They were often asked within the group if they ever played in the movies... Moose was plump also, but very tall and was, of course, much more muscular of all the other committee members...

The quintet of searchers asked the deities to warp them together to Gliese-667Cc. But before the warp, Moose submitted a wish to the Deities: He asked them to warp them directly to the most suitable earth-like planet. Unfortunately, no planet appeared before them. The Deities felt that **serial** warping is best for their disciples. This way they will learn to accept even planets defective in one or two parameters and to terraform them. Did they know that the eleven planets that the committee chose (the ten planets of Jordan and the planet that John recommended), were defective in one parameter or two? With a sigh, Moose acknowledged the Deities' decision.

This this is what the committee found on Gliese-667Cc It was indeed an exoplanet that is apparently very far from Earth, since it was in the Milky Way galaxy, but very far from Terra. Both John and Jordan could only recognize one or two of the biggest stars of the Milky way galaxy. Since Gliese-667 was very far from Terra, it fits the important parameter that Moose stipulated – as far away from the "earthies" of Terra, as possible.

The Gliese-667Cc planet orbits around Gliese 667C, a small red dwarf. It appeared to orbit much closer to the red dwarf than that of Earth's orbit around Sol (Earth's sun). Still, the important finding was that Gliese-667Cc planet receives a similar amount of energy from its star as Earth receives from SOL. Therefore, its atmospheric temperature is temperate, and suitable for their habitation.

To determine whether the planet's atmosphere has good air for Human breathing, both Moose and the group's atmosphere analyzer, Bill, asked their Deities to make a small opening in their two cells. They wanted to quickly sample the atmospheric air. They took a cautious sniff and immediately approved the quality of the air, as suitable for Human breathing. After their "sniff" they asked the Deities to close back the cell. They reported the result to the astronomers but cautioned them not to breathe the air yet, lest it contains some toxic element. They lied down, prepared to call their Deities for medical help in case of a toxic response. No toxic response manifested itself.

So far, their visit to Gliese has been a success with regards to the air and the temperature. They needed to test one additional important parameter: Water. In their cursory inspection, walking around the cells' areas, they did not see any sea, river or spring. If, for instance, there had been a sea, even a very salty or poisonous one, they could have asked the Deities for an automatic desalination plant...

Moose and friends warped around the whole plane and failed to find any water sources that were open to the atmosphere. Therefore, the water specialist, Clark, went back to his cell and came out with a short wooden stick wrapped in cloth. He unwrapped it and said: "Please guys, do not laugh! I am going to use a very antiquated technic that we learned from our ancient ancestors". He pointed to the stick and said: "This is a dousing rod. If there is water below the ground, then when I touch the rod to the ground,, my **hand** feels vibrations. The stick itself does not vibrate". His companions looked askance at him, but did not say anything. Clark stuck the rod into several sites distant from each other and looked with a critical eye for any hand-vibrations. Then he addressed Moose and the other three committee members and told them: "there is water at a depth of twenty feet in many places all over the planet". Then he told Moose that he needs a medium-sized oilrig to unearth the water.

Moose did not believe that the "dousing" act would work, but despairingly acquiesced, and he himself addressed the Deities. In seconds, a drill with all its attachments appeared. Clark asked his friends to help him, under his instruction. All five men worked hard for two days, and when they reached a depth of eighteen feet, they heard a rumble in the Earth. Clark laughed happily and removed his comrades from the vicinity of the site. Immediately, the drilling pipe burst out of the rig and flew in the air like a rocket. In its wake burst a huge fountain of clear water! The councilors cupped some water in their hands and cautiously tasted it. It was the sweetest water that they had ever tasted. After all, during their life on Terra, the quality of water was already terribly bad unless it was chemically purified.

Highly gratified, and quite assured, Clark grabbed some water in a bottle and entered his cell, where he had a complete organic, biologic and unorganic analytical laboratory. He ran a sample from the fountain-water through his many retorts. But instead of being happy, his face turned slightly grey. He analyzed a second and a third sample and received an identical result each time. He called his four comrades and sadly informed them that the water has a serious flaw – a case of "a fly in the ointment"... He identified in the planet's water a compound very similar to a Human Female Hormone called Progesterone." It may not interest you", he said. "But it has the chemical formula $C_{21}H_{30}O_2$." It is an estrogen that is active in female reproduction and has a terrible "feminization" effect on Human males. It is completely forbidden for males.

Moose almost cried in desperation, but then calmed-down and said "I thought that we may have a case of beginners' luck. But no matter! There are many more fish in the ocean, and many more candidate planets to warp to!" They returned to the whole group and did not inform the group of the results. But because the committee did not say anything, the group understood that the first warp was unsuccessful. He did not inform the group of the reason. As a leader, he felt that he should tell the group only the barest minimum...

Second and a third warping attempts

For an additional warp, Moose remembered that Jordan recommended to warp serially through his list of the ten most earth-like planets. But the disappointment with Gliese-667Cc caused him to jump straight to John's recommendation: Kepler 186f planet.

True to john's first theoretical description of "his" exoplanet, the search committee found the following attributes for Kepler 186f:

It was indeed a far exoplanet in the Milky Way because, as before, the astronomers recognized only one or two of the Milky Way's stars. Kepler 186f circles a red dwarf star called Kepler 186 (without the 'f'). It has a "habitable zone" that allows its planets to receive a perfect amount of heat to maintain liquid water on their surfaces, and so it also has a temperate air-temperature. Its atmospheric air was sweet and non-toxic. By a first approximation It looked to them a twin of the earth.

In their first cursory inspection outside their cells, they saw an extremely "watery" planet!! So that an important requirement for Humans – **water**, was fulfilled. Their warp landed their cells inside a riverbed of a large spring!

This time, all five members of the delegation sprang out and tasted the water. But they had to filter sand from the water to taste it. They did this by first filtering the muddy water through filter paper, and then through a 0.1-micron filter. When they tasted the water, they found that it was slightly salty. Clark subjected the water through the retorts of his analytical instrument and told his companions that the water contains only a low concentration of one mineral – Magnesium chloride. Magnesium chloride salt is important for Human health. Clark also gladly informed them that the water is completely innocuous – it is devoid of any hormones and does not contain any proteins or sugars. Moose embraced Clark and told him that the previous "goodies" that were withheld from him after the Gliese's sorry result (although it was not really his fault) - are reinstated…

"Evening" according to the Kepler 186 star came and the star stopped to shed its light. A thick pillow of clouds appeared in the sky and the temperature, and the barometer, dropped quickly. Then the clouds started to vent their antipathy for the planet (Only God or the Deities know why…). They poured down hundreds of cubic feet of rain. In a very short time, about seven feet height of water covered the whole planet and the cells!!

The sad five companions quickly hid in their cells. Again, Moose was affected most of all of them, and opened his mouth to say something but Clark preceded him and said: "I know… I know…for this lousy planet I do not deserve any benefits…"

Following their two failures to find a suitable home planet, the comrades felt that they are now more experienced. However, they were now afraid that they would, finally, need to terraform because in all of Jordan's list there may be only "defective" planets.

Now they returned serially again to the second place in Jordan's list but their third warp: – to Kepler-22b. When they warped, they landed in along rocky channel filled with water to a height of about 15 inches. They tasted the sweet transparent water from the channel and waited for a toxic reaction that, luckily, did not come.

Clark quickly grabbed a cup of the water and passed it through his dependable instrument. He waited with shaking hands for the necessary time, jumped to the cell's computer and wildly tore its output. Finally, he could tell his friends again that the water was without any hormones or other organic dangerous contaminants!

After his analysis in his instrument, Clark looked around and saw that their tested channel was just one of an ordered system spreading lengthwise and sideways as far as the eye could see.

Clark picked up a telescope to see how far the channels went. Then breathing heavily, he cried: "Indians, Indians, look!" When the "Indians" came closer, the committee saw that the Indigenous "Indians" were large hives of arthropods like Terran grasshoppers. As the arthropods came closer, the comrades saw that in their hands (legs?) they held sharp spears! The five explorers jumped into their cells and warped off.

The committee did not report to the group in what they failed. This time, however, the discovery of indigenous beings was so striking that they had to tell about them to their group!

A successful fourth warping tor an earth-like planet and preliminary attempts to settle down

Very insistently, the five comrades warped to the serial third choice in Jordan's list: Kepler-69c. It was to be their fourth warped planet (the second warp to Kepler 186f interfered in their orderly list choices). After all, they did not have any choice. It is true that they could warp, at random, to any Planet in the Milky Way galaxy. But they felt that Jordan's list was still their best bet. Because up to this minute, the committee had three failures out of three planets, Jordan prepared a form that will characterize each planet. The form contained all the information that they currently had on the previous planets:

Name of planet:
Name of star:
Habitable zone:
Water quality:
Taste:
Presence of toxicity:
Presence of Hormones:
Air quality:
Atmospheric air components:
Mount of rain:
Presence of indigenous life:

Jordan thought that since the form contains all their good results up to now (with the exception of the indigenous grasshoppers, it may bring them more luck... (he was slightly superstitious...).

After the comrades warped to Kepler-69c, this is how their completed form looked:

Name of Planet	Kepler-69c
Name of Star	Kepler 69
Habitable zone	Present
Water quality: 　　Taste: 　　Presence of toxicity: 　　Presence of hormone:	 Sweet None None
Air quality	Very good
Atmospheric air components	Nitrogen, Oxygen, Neon
Amount of rain	Moderate
Presence of indigenous life	none

The committee looked at Jordan's form and were happy. They did not really have to look at the results in the form, because they were already aware of them in reality! They knew, however, that a failure may nevertheless still appear.

The group's betrayal and a forced warping

For quite some time, the group waited breathlessly and impatiently to settle down on a planet that they can call "Home". When Moose notified them that they can finally warp to Kepler-69c, they went crazy with joy. A big immigration started and was complete twenty-four later. Once on the planet, they left their cells, sang and danced happily in the streets. (The "streets" were formed by the orderly rows of cells that the group placed). The songs were mostly favorites from their old earth. But the dances were their own crazy improvisations.,

At the beginning, all the cells warped together to a small area (the "streets"). They wanted to find safety in numbers, although Moose assured them that Kepler-69c is completely safe. But then, their old Yankee independence asserted itself, and more and more independent souls started to disperse further and further. They Wanted to be free of their aggregation in the large cells' camp of the "streets" … Also, Moose told them that Kepler-69c may not be their destination, because the committee may continue with their searches, with additional and more rigorous parameters (this was despite the good parameters of Kepler 69c…) Therefore, they felt free to roam until the time for the next warp would arrive (or anyway stay on the present safe planet).

Before, in the large cells' camp, antipathies, sympathies and even love ran free., despite the compressed placement of the cells. Now, unchecked, people combined two or even more cells to "celebrate" in faraway places! In some cases, Moose as the leader (the mayor…), even had to officiate in formal weddings!

It should be said that Moose, a liberal mayor, quite wisely, did not interrupt the "celebrations". One additional thing that he did not do: he did not distribute birth-control pills… As a matter of fact, he wanted his community to have babies and to grow.

Some of his people, especially past builders and stonemasons started to **exercise** cutting building stones from the stony Kepler-69c,

Moose was quite unhappy with the dispersion of his people. He was afraid that once the people were completely free to roam, they may like it so much on the present planet that they would not return to the fold. Indeed, he saw many people (even some from his most trusted councilors' committee) drifting in all the compass' directions. He was afraid that he would be left with only a small remnant of his group. However, he could do nothing to stop his people's desertion. His title of "leader' was an honorary one that he received because of his far-seeing ability. It did not give him any real ruling privileges.

In view of the betrayal of many of "his" people, he felt like he was partaking a role in the famous Latin proverb: "Sic transit gloria mundi" ("thus passes the glory of the world" – meaning "Fame is fleeing"). He even, sadly, thought to change his name to Gloria… Fortunately, soon his luck was going to change for the better:

A planet's period, like "Spring" in some lucky Terran regions, had arrived. Some settlers in far-away areas planted Terran seedlings that they brought with them from Terra. They wanted to start their own small terraforming orchards. After all, the committee of five told them that Kepler 69c was free of any indigenous life. Therefore, they were unpleasantly surprised to see huge swarms of flying "insects", surrounding their seedlings. They looked a lot like Terran wasps. But the diet of Terran leaves did not please the "palates" of the "insects" and they tried to lick, and then stung the unhappy people. 'Unhappy", because those who were stung, developed high fever and aching muscles. The Deities had a lot of work to cure them. All The widespread people, who betrayed their "heritage" and left Moose behind, rushed to their cells and warped back to the "cell park". They were surprised that Moose freely accepted them back to the fold, without any punishment. They did not know that he was happy that they had come back at all.

As a result of the indigenous "wasps", all the people warped from Kepler 69c in a hurry and waited in space for happier results from the committee.

A fifth warping

The "committee of five" geared their loins and warped to Kepler-62f, the fourth planet in Jordan's list. They hoped that this time, finally, it may be a good Earth-like planet.

Moose knew that Many thinkers such as Shakespeare, Voltaire and others already said that "always striving for the **better**, will keep us from appreciating of the **good** that we already have". He was ready to accept even a "lame, one-leg" planet and terraform it.

The committee, by virtue of their previous reticence, did not feel a need to tell their people of the possible terraforming plan for fear that it may elicit long and futile discussions without reaching any conclusion. But all the group relied on Moose, and they knew that when the committee left for a new search, they recently started to report their results at the end of each search.

The group also knew that the search committee members were risking their life in searches of unknown planets that may hold very dangerous surprises. Therefore, they did not pester them for descriptions of the failed searches if they did not see the failures with their own eyes (like indigent life..). The experienced committee quickly performed the testing of Kepler-62f. They even worked as single examiners that divided the workload between them. In a very few hours since they started, they finished their searching and convened to fill Jordan's test form.

One by one they filled out their results, and when they looked at the filled form, they felt that they were finally successful. This was the filled form for Kepler 62f:

Name of the tested planet:	Kepler-62f
Name of Star:	Kepler 62
Habitable zone:	Present

Water quality:
    Taste:
    Presence of toxicity, or
    hormones:
	excellent
	None

Air quality	very good
Atmospheric air components	80% nitrogen, 16% oxygen, 4% noble gases: Neon, Helium and a new one that Clark labeled as Xenomium after the Earth's Xenon
Amount of dew at night	1 liter per 1 square yard
Presence of indigenous life: Dangerous to Humans:	They ignore Humans
Volume of rain per 24 hours:	Five liters per square yard
Is the earth rocky or easily arable?	Mostly easily arable
Land flat or hilly:	Hilly in some places, flat in others

The failing of Kepler 62f

The committee s notified the group that they may have a good planet for them. Still, learning from what happened with Kepler 69c, they qualified the results by warning the group not to rejoice before time.

However, most of the group were already too impatient and like the case of Kepler 69c, a big immigration started again and was complete twenty-four later.

As before, they left their cells and sang happily in the streets... But remembering their previous failed immigrations, this time they did not dance. At the start they were still leery. But then their optimism soared, and many independent souls started again to disperse further and further.

Moose tried to save them from further disappointment in case of an additional failure and told them **again** that Kepler-62f may not be their destination because the committee is going to continue with their search. Therefore, it is better for them to wait, he said. But as before, they did not heed him. They felt free to roam again.

In the first three days no mishap happened, and they were ready to go on with their life on Kepler 62f. They were very happy with the good arability of great plots on the planet, which they started to plow.

But after three days they began, during the workdays of plowing, to yawn more and more. When they talked about this "yawning" phenomenon with their neighbors, they realized that their tiredness was due to terrible nightmares that filled their sleep. As the nights went on, the nightmares grew in intensity. Moose was confronted with a great volume of complaints and urgently assembled his entire committee to try to solve the problem.

However, the committee was completely stymied. Finally,

the air specialist and analyst Bill, who was very reticent and unassuming, popped up and said: "I was hoping that aside from me, someone else knew the answer, but nobody did. So, unfortunately, now it fell to me to tell you what is happening: In my air analyses I discovered a **new** noble gas that Terra does not have. I named this gas "Xenomium" by virtue of its resemblance to the Terran Xenon.

I analyzed large amounts of Kepler 62f's air and isolated a pure amount of Xenomium from the air. Then I wore a gas mask from which I pumped out all breathable air and replaced its former air with purified Xenomium. In about five minutes I was struck with a terrible headache, and nightmares flew through my brain even without any sleep!" Now, at the very least, the whole committee understood the reason for their nightmares! And although this knowledge did not help them to procure the planet, all of them stood up, clapped their hands and congratulated Bill for solving the terrible mystery. Moose clasped Bill's hand in gratitude and granted him a large package of "goodies"! Bill distributed the goodies, anyway, to the committee. But they did not help the whole group…

The seventh warp

The committee warped to the next planet in Jordan's list. As before in their recent testings, the committee members split, and each had his unique list of parameters to test.

When the results of all four committee members were entered in the form, this is how it looked:

Name of the tested planet:	Kepler-442b
Name of Star:	Kepler 442
Habitable zone:	Present
Air quality	very good
Atmospheric air components	80% nitrogen, 16% oxygen, 4% noble gases: Neon, Helium, Krypton
Amount of dew at night	1 liter per 1 square yard
Volume of rain per 24 hours:	five liters per square yard
Is the earth rocky or easily arable?	Mostly arable
Type of land:	Large plots of red loam interspersed between brown earth that is very fertile for the growth of all grains,
Presence of indigenous life:	Yes, but They ignore Humans

Once again, committee members were satisfied with the results until they remembered that several planets before, the results were promising at first sight, until some very bad trouble popped up and destroyed their early optimism!

The committee members wanted at first to notify the group that they may have a good planet for them. Still, learning from what happened with Kepler 62f and other promising planets, they decided that they do not want to disappoint their group again because of an unexpected "boo-boo".

The committee decided to hide the apparent good results from the group. They were afraid that a dispersal into the planet would end again in a fast warp to space. Finally, Moose, who was afraid of a revolt that will depose him in case of a bad trouble again, came up with a solution: He suggested to reveal secretly the good results to a group of fifty mature, intelligent men, who could warp to the planet with their wives and live there for a month in various places. The committee will also supervise them. Their whole group in space would surely assume that the committee is currently missing for a whole month because they are consecutively studying more planets, one after the other.

Meanwhile, the "spies" lived happily on Kepler 442b, plowing large arable plots for sowing at the beginning of the planet's rainy season. Moreover, with the committee's approval they meditated to the Deities for templates that were to be used to produce red loam bricks for home-building! Red loam was present in large amounts all over the planet. They were very successful in producing the bricks and also meditated on many more **ready** bricks which were very generously supplied by the Deities. They even received various dyes that they incorporated into the loam to produce artful designs that they built into colorful model houses!

At the end of thirty days, the "spies" delivered a unanimous verdict: "bring all the sad multitudes of our group to the planet! We did not encounter any danger in the whole planet!" Based on the spies' opinion, and on their own observations, the Committee happily agreed. They warped to the group's camp and brought them the happy tidings.

Within just a few hours, (and not within 24 hours as before), the whole group quickly warped to Kepler 442b. They wanted to grab the best arable plots to settle. They also wanted to plow and to build houses like those of the "spies". They used their cells to mark their domains until the time would come to build houses. Each domain was situated within a limit of five hundred acres that Moose decreed. Moose managed to maintain his leadership by establishing a police force to monitor plot-size deviations. However, he mitigated the harshness of his decree by saying that after all the group will be **concentrated in one city,** they can warp to possess additional lots of plots all over the planet! The crafty thinking-ahead Moose already planned to establish elections in which he would figure mightily! Moreover, many people established love and sex relations as couples, threesomes and foursomes, during their roaming between planets. (The primal urge for intimacy and sex worked also in ex-ghosts after their solidifications)!

Many people needed to change places with the immediate neighbors of their love-objects, which managed to precede them in occupying a plot near their loved ones. Moose employed his police to help the people to live near their lovers and gained favors that he knew that he would ask for their repayment in the future election that planned to run.

Moose did not have a sweetheart, although he could have picked several beautiful ladies that eyed him with favor. He was quite obsessed with his political ambitions, and therefore did not build a family house. Instead, with other confirmed bachelors like him, he oversaw the building of public houses. A governor house, a Capitol, etc. (hopefully for himself...)

The Deities bid farewell

As described, Moose occupied himself in erecting public buildings. Part of it was easy – meditation and "so long, good-bye and thanks" to the Deities. But slowly a gradual change occurred. Little by little the Deities failed to deliver meditation requests, until the supply dried out completely.

Then one day a single Deity assembled the whole group (even the children) and out of a loudspeaker, **without any appearance,** he "said: "Dear group, despite our wish, my brothers and I must leave you. During the recent time that I helped you, you came very nicely of age and progressed very well, especially with Moose as your leader. You are a group which we treated with great satisfaction, and we are sorry to leave. However, we must attend to other groups who grow rapidly in number. Aside from the conventional mode of dying because of old age or a disease, **more dead people than usual** need our attention. This is because of terrible wars that are fought all over earth! To name just a few; Ukraine against Russia, the army of the Sudan against the SPLA liberation army, Israel against the terrorists, the dead citizens in the Gaza strip, etc. etc. Therefore, I and my co-workers must, against our wishes, leave you! We can only say goodbye and wish you good luck!

Moose raised his voice, trying to get some reprieve, but the loudspeaker had already disappeared! The whole group mourned for one day, but Moose consoled them and encouraged them to take it like men (and women).

Because of the desertion of the Deities, who till now helped him and his builders, Moose had to shift the emphasis of his building enterprises. He needed to enroll the colonists in **group building jobs**. Therefore, he established a 'shift program' for all the group's able men and women. All of them were very strong and could contribute much to the new group's buildings enterprise.

Moose prepared a list of building priorities as follows:

1. Production and drying of large stocks of bricks of red loam in the molds that the Deities supplied them with before they left. At that time, they also still supplied the group with thousands and thousands of bricks, many sacs of cement, wooden doors and window frames. One of the men of the group knew how to forge glass, and Moose mobilized him to produce glass panes throughout the whole building period. Moose, of course, had to discard his intention of building municipal buildings because there were more critical group jobs.

2. A general and surgical hospital: Due to the past generosity of their Deities, the surgeons and GPs in the group were well equipped with surgical equipment and medical supplies that they took good care of. The doctors were young ones who died of diseases or in surgery, so that they were still qualified, and were elated to fulfil again their curing role in life instead of the Deities. Also, there were many qualified nurses who died because of a psycho bombing in a large hospital.

3. A nursery and kindergarten for the babies so that their mothers could join the building enterprises

4. A communal cowshed and milking station for the grown babies.

5. Brick homes for all people, couples of lovers, etc.

6. A dairy for producing milk products

7. A mill for wheat and a communal bakery.

8. A repair shop for agricultural implements

9. A gas station - Extending the current small station. Several months ago, Moose asked their water specialist and analyst, Clark, to "douse" for oil. Clark made several trials that ended in several water wells which the group needed. He finally also found a location with underground oil. Two months ago, before the Deities left, Clark asked them for a small refinery to isolate gasoline from crude oil. This was the last machine that settlers received from their Deities...

Most of the early enterprises were built on a small scale that now required enlarging. in one month, all the projects were complete and assured the group that they could survive without the help of their Deities. The group celebrated the completion of the projects for 2 whole days!

How can we help the failed-reincarnated communities?

After the group finished feasting and carousing on a glass of milk (they did not have any alcohol yet), one women from the group asked Moose the following Question: "Hi dear Moose, if my poor memory serves me right, I seem to remember that some time ago you said that once we find us a good planet and build our homes, you will warp to earth to help failed reincarnated communities - teach them to solidify and to warp. We have a lot of free space in our planet, so that we can invite them to live with us…

Moose pretended to think about her question and hit his forehead in a sign that he had completely forgotten this promise. All the people in the feast burst out laughing and some of them almost choked up. The questioning woman laughed too assuming that all people laughed at the comic way that moose hit himself!

Moose added to the hilarity further by saying: "Wow, how could I forget such an important thing!" But then he remembered that the woman is in the early throes of Alzheimer, and gently reminded her: "Dear Bertha, I cannot warp to earth because the deities left us! They were the only ones who could warp us". Bertha thought for some time and said: "Is that so? Oh,then I am sorry that I asked".

Then Moose addressed his people and said: "Bertha sometimes has a little trouble remembering things. After all, she is 90 years old, and did not want to bother the Deities for her slight problem". All the group, ashamed, immediately stopped laughing.

The next day, a loudspeaker appeared in the center of the red (and differently colorful) city. The people of the group assumed that the Deities wanted to congratulate them on the finished buildings and gathered around the loudspeaker. The deity on the "speaking duty" said: "Hi there my most favorite group in the whole world. And hi there to your excellent mayor Moose! I want to congratulate you on the beautiful building job that you all performed!" The group gratefully accepted the congratulations and some of them turned to leave. But then the Deity added: "Please do not leave yet. I have something more to tell you!"

Then the Deity said: "You remember that when I explained why we must leave you, I told you that we were overworked because of the increase of warfare in the world? Now we are facing the worst ever situation, and we almost decided not to reincarnate Humanity anymore! We were completely overwhelmed by the amount of work! However, by some chance, we listened to innocent Bertha and reached a solution! Here it is: In the Old Testament that was composed by one of our God-bosses and very talented human authors and poets, there is a sentence in the book of Psalms: It goes like this in free translation - "from the mouth of suckling babies I learned to exhibit valor to vanquish my enemies!!" To wit: From dear innocent Bertha we learned that we need to mobilize you, "babies", to help us!" We helped you all along, so that you are now extremely qualified and smart and there are many of you. We implore you to marshal yourselves and help us to teach the reincarnated humans in their caverns! Warp to all the caverns that contain the reincarnated people, and teach them to meditate, solidify, and warp! Then ask them to join your "instruction Platoon". Because you helped them, they will feel grateful, and join your "platoons" and will teach other reincarnated people in the thousands of caverns to solidify, etc. This way, by a geometrical progression, our "instruction platoons" will increase tremendously in number and finish the job in no time!"

Moose and his group clapped hands and shouted "Halleluja"! Then Moose said: "Dear Deity, surely there are additional groups like ours on other planets in the Milky way who can, together with us, join the instruction project?" The deity answered: "Dear Moose, my heart is grieving because I must tell you that we . reincarnated thousands of caverns. However, only you and your group, because of your science-fiction knowledge, learned how to solidify and warp! Unfortunately, our bosses, the Gods, set up a code that does not allow us to address reincarnated people **of our volition**, unless they specifically meditate and require "favors" from us! We think that you and your group are the greatest, but this is also because we have no other developed group like yours!! You are incomparable!!"! The deity said this with a weeping voice. Moose answered, sadly, because he grieved for "their" Deity: "Sure! we shall help you with all our powers". The Deity thanked the group heartily, this time with a happy voice because of Moose's agreement, and joined, sight unseen, the merriment of the building-feast . Several hours later, he finally disappeared with his loudspeaker.

The group allocated some men to take care of the major hard jobs in the colorful city. Even muscular older women who were not breastfeeding, joined the city's interim maintenance team.

The volunteers of Moose' "instruction platoon" divided among themselves the countries of the world according to their language proficiencies. When they warped to countries which they did not know their languages, they received help from Deities: The Deities used a psychological method known as Hypnopedia (sleep teaching). This is an instruction of a sleeping person by recorded lessons. It works well, but the Deities used their "magic" to speed up many fold the learning capacity.

The "missionaries" of the group saw a lot of success in establishing more and more "sub"- and "sub-sub" missionaries". Half a year later, their instruction work and that of their sub groups was complete so that they were all free to tour to all the great marvels of earth. They went to great shows, ate in several

excellent restaurants. Occasionally, since they were without their
wives, they even frequented the best whorehouses relying on the
deities to cure them from any diseases that they might contract...
After a long time in the pleasure pots (or spots) of the world, little
by little they returned home.

For quite some time, the name that the town on Kepler
442b acquired was the "town of moose". This was when in
when in municipal elections, Moose was elected mayor (he was
the only candidate). Then, because the name was too long and
cumbersome, an elected city-council changed it to "Moosustown"
and then again to **Moosus**. All this happened before the "big
bang" event, which was the name that the group assigned to the
Deities' instruction plea.

The great migration of the reincarnated people

The returning "missionaries" huddled in various school halls for discussions. Finally, after their discussions, they chose a few fluent people to meet with Moose and his city council. Moose welcomed them and thanked them for their great job on Terra. But they did not come for praise. they had some agenda mind: they entered the council hall wishing to raise the subject of the poor living conditions of the poor reincarnated people that they rescued from the caverns... but before they said anything, Moose preceded them and said: "Dear missionaries! I know what you came to say. You and us in Moosus are facing a great crisis, and I had been aware of it from Day one". Then he turned to both his council and the missionaries and said: "our planet is completely overrun with myriads of poor reincarnated warped fugitives from Terra, and their number is growing each day. A very large fragment of our city's yearly budget goes now just to feed them and teach reincarnated children, and nothing more.. They are now a huge welfare community.

I meditated and applied to our Deities, which we so diligently, just recently, helped and I begged them to find us a much bigger and fertile planet for the new reincarnateds and to take care of them on the new planet that they would find for them. I am waiting now, breathlessly, for their response". Moose's words were suddenly interrupted by some functionary who whispered something in his ear. Moose stopped talking to the council and the missionaries and said that he must stop the meeting now for a while. The people in the meeting hall watched through the windows .moose's steps out the council hall. they saw a loudspeaker standing in the town's center...

Moose came back with a happy face. He told the gathering that the Deities found a very large, and fertile planet in the Milky Way galaxy. Moose said that the deity he talked to, said that the planet's surface area is 20 times greater than that of Kepler 442b. The Deities will warp once to the planet to direct the new reincarnateds where to warp, and Hallelujah! They will care for all the fugitives' needs. When Moose finished speaking, the roof of the council hall almost broke because of the peoples' happy shouts of joy.

The fact that Moose was the mayor that sent his men to teach the reincarnates in their caverns, and that a Deity chose to speak only to him, raised his stature among all Humans in the new planet... Moose did not leave anything to chance and made sure that all the new immigrants to the new plant would learn about his great move on their behalf. He was now obsessed again with political ambition, and He wanted to be elected to the highest post in the new planet to become its new president. As a first step, he suggested a name for the new planet – "Resurrection". This name symbolized the new condition that all the new Terran reincarnateds now found themselves.

It should be recalled that moose did not marry, although several pretty and young ladies tried to "snare" him". Occasionally, he did have some unimportant meeting of "belly to belly" encounters, but did not commit himself. As was already indicated, he was now obsessed by politics. He realized that it was still too early to start a presidential election when the new citizens of "resurrection" needed time to recover from their previous hardships. But he still made some campaigning like introducing himself as the leader who helped them through his men, and also by kissing the immigrant orphan babies.

The Deities provided the new immigrants to Resurrection with all their needs. But it was necessary to make them self-sufficient as soon as possible. Therefore, all the members of Mooses' councilor committee decided warp to Resurrection to teach the "natives" their respective professions as soon as there would be enough reincarnates on Resurrection.

Moose stands for election

Moose and two members of his erstwhile councilor committee went to Resurrection to orient the community of the new immigrants to the planet of Resurrection. These poor people were still confused and disoriented, as they were in their caverns before their warp - in a split second their life turned over. True, the Deities supplied everything that they needed, but what they lacked most at present was adequate orientation - Some people who could explain to them how their life on the planet will progress. Moose and the two other volunteers divided between them the various places around the planet in which they held large orientation meetings and seminars. Moose was the most active among them. Where the other two volunteers held two or three meetings per day, Moose held four to six seminars daily, for half a year. This was much longer than the two other volunteers. These two other volunteers were married, and after a while missed their families and warped back. Also, with his stature of six feet and large bulk he made a very strong impression on the immigrants that he oriented.

At the end of every meeting, Moose propagandized. He told the grateful listeners that he oversaw the missionaries who saved them and asked them, unashamedly, to remember him when the election-time for president of Resurrection will happen. Moose also persuaded the committee members in charge of Resurrection that such an election could stiffen with pride the backs of immigrants from democratic countries. He meant mostly English-speaking people that he mostly instructed.

As a result of a lot of pestering from Moose, who was after all, their mayor on their own planet, the council finally agreed to hold elections.

The committee asked the Deities to supply them with thousands of ballot boxes and instruct English speaking immigrants (the major language in Terra) through hypnopedia to act as ballot officers and to strengthen the knowledge of those were not fluent enough. Moose also persuaded the committee that the election should be held in English which was, after all, the most prevalent language on Resurrection.

A call for candidates was issued in English by the Deities' loudspeakers. Not very surprisingly, the new confused reincarnates did not care to compete with the single registered strong candidate (Moose).

After counting the ballots, which encompassed fifteen percent of all reincarnates - lo and behold, Moose was elected as president of Resurrection. Moose resigned his post as the mayor of Moosus and Clark was elected in his stead.

Moose warps to Saint Louis

After his election as the president of Resurgence, Moose warped in the middle of the night to Saint-Louis. He had his reasons: Saint -Louis is among the most dangerous cities in the United States. It has about 14 Murders per 100,000 people every year.

With the help of his Deities, Moose was warped to a cavern filled with murderers. That first cavern had expert murderers who died because of fighting another gang of murderers on the control of an area. Naturally, the opposing gang also had representatives in the cavern. When Moose entered to the cavern, he raised his bass-voice and said: "Hi dear men! Listen to me! I am a president of a very large planet in the milky Way. It does not have milk but stupid immigrants that I want to exploit. I had been a "goody-goody" person up to now but there is no profit in it! Therefore, I want to start a Mafia group on the new planet and exploit its stupid people. I know how to reach the planet by flying in a new method which I will use to bring all my mafia group, numbering 100 strong, and are expert killers to the planet. The flight to the island will be performed for us by stupid god-like (or better still Witch-like) characters that I call Deities. They are under my control and do what I tell them.

Moose continued: "Now, those among you had the expertise to kill somebody, and not be killed himself, please raise your hand." Seventeen hands were raised. Among them was one of the "killers" that proposed himself as a murderer, but he actually was not a murderer, but a **murdered** person called Piotr. He pretended to be a killer because he **"smelled"** that it will be his passport out of the cavern...

Then Moose continued: "does anybody here have a secret Cache of weapons? I shall buy them to equipe our new mafia".

One criminal hesitantly raised his hand and confided that he has a cache with a lot of Thompson Sub-machine guns in top condition. He said that they were kept well-oiled, and that his cache also contains many cartridges and magazines. He also added that he would be glad to sell them cheaply to the Boss. Moose could have asked the Deities for the weapons, but he wanted to obtain the confidence of his new Mafia group by buying weapons for them.

Moose ordered the criminals to stay meantime in the cavern, since he wants to enlist more men from other caverns and then all of them will fly with him to the new planet. He planned to rule its inhabitants by force of fear and weapons. He told his mafiosos that the new flight method, "warping," is instantaneous. He told the cache-owner to bring the weapons to the assembly cavern and divide them among the mafiosos.

The "herding" of additional criminals to reach a group of hundred went quickly. Moose **ordered** the Deities to warp all the killer group to a big hall in his presidential palace in Resurrection. This was his council room which he obliterated. Moose did not need to meditate to ask the Deities. He saw that they docilly complied with all his orders (they owed Moose for orchestrating their freedom from their previous impossibly difficult reincarnated work).

The president issues new decrees

Moose ordered from the Deities policemen's uniforms for his killer-mafiosos. The Deities were also forced to feed the "policemen" and to do their laundry. They also supplied the "policemen" with 100 beds, which they placed in the big ex-council hall.

Next he issued new printed presidential decrees (printed by the Deities) as follows:

1. "The name of the planet will be "**Mooses' empire**" and not any other stupid name that had been suggested by someone else. All new presidential paperwork shall bear this new name and my own name: "The illustrious Moses" or "the illustrious Moose."

2. "All citizens shall transfer to my treasury any Dollars that they may have carried with them during their reincarnation and solidification. My policemen have my permission to search your tents" (the whole populace had to erect cloth tents to live in). They thought, originally, as Clark's men told them, that they will build for themselves brick houses. But Clark's men were completely unaware of the ugly Empire that moose instigated! They were busy incorporating new lucky reincarnateds to their Moosus' island).

3. "Parents, if you have daughters that have died with you, you must supply them to me. I want a beautiful new virgin every week. I shall impregnate the virgins and eventually will add the born boys, when they grow up, to my police".

4. "My empire needs gold. I, myself, will tell you where it can be found. In the places that I indicate (the Deities had to tell him...) you will have to start mines that will be

operated by strong young guys who will be also mobilized to serve in the army that I shall establish. The length of their service would be Five years. Deserters from either the mine, or the military service will be shot forthwith".

Moose wanted the gold to guild his palace on the outside, and its toilets and its baths on the inside. He also had sculptors among his citizens prepare many big golden busts of his six feet image. To fulfil his caprices, he established many deep mines that cost the lives of many young unhappy recruits!.

Emperor Moose continues with his oppression

The reincarnateds that were warped to live in "Moose's empire" contained people from all walks of life – from municipal garbage collectors, which performed a scoffed-at, smelly and necessary service, up to senators and legislators. They were solidified and warped to the big Empire planet with the heart-felt and best wishes of the citizens of Moosus and their sub- and sub-subdivisions. Therefore, they were hopeful that they are going to live happily in a new reincarnateds' large planet.

Imagine their surprise and disappointment, when instead of going to live in new brick houses like the citizens of Moosus' various "subs" own houses, they were pushed to live in cloth tents with other families. At least they were well-fed by the deities, and the children, who were not necessarily part of their families, received schooling. Other than that, they quickly learned that they fell under the rule of a gross and cruel dictator. They realized that they do not live in Paradise, but in partial Hell! The young people among them were drafted to work in dangerous mines, and in an army about to go to war against a much smaller island – Moosus, that they knew is under the protection of omnipotent Deities!

It did not take much time for the reincarnateds to unite the inferior-station and the superior-station undergrounds. This was in addition to earlier established undergrounds.

However, All the members of the undergrounds suffered from a terrible handicap: they did not have any weapons whatsoever. They could not revolt with bare hands. At least they had the presence of mind to unite.

Unfortunately, things in the Empire came to a head: The underground learned from its "mole" – a Russian policeman named Piotr Klachkin, that moose is going to war against Musson: he plans to send to war many of the young miners, commanded by his policemen as officers. The mole Piotr was a Russian ex-spy who was caught spying and executed in Washington, in retaliation for an American agent executed by Putin's henchmen. He was lucky to be reincarnated into the murderers' cavern from which moose mobilized his policemen. By pretending to be a murderer he was warped to Moose's empire. Piotr told the underground leaders that the miners will be armed with rifles containing only 5 bullets in a magazine, against the Moosus' soldiers that will be armed with the most modern weapons that their Deities can supply. As one of the policemen to which the emperor lectured and motivated, he told the underground leaders that Moose plans to sacrifice his young miners and replace them with new ones!

Piotr was a Bolshevik in his past and he learned during his past indoctrination about the heroic revolt of the "Potemkin". Potemkin was a dreadnought battleship built for the imperial Russian navy in the black sea. It is best remembered for its 1905 mutiny by its communist sailors. The mutiny failed, but its heroic fight stayed in the popular soviet memory. Among the leaders of the underground was a history professor that verified Piotr's story and asked him why he brought the story.

Piotr answered that the underground ought to try to raise a mutiny among the young miners so that they will not try to kill Moosus' army and be killed by them instead. The professor liked Piotr's idea, recommended it, and the underground decided to act on it. It assigned some of their adults to incite the young miners.

Unfortunately, until the slow underground reacted, the miners were warped to Moosus! Holding their sticks (primitive rifles…), they aimed them at the Moosus' army. But, where the Moosus' army formation was just a second ago, was now just air. The poor miners' army repeated their aiming maneuver and again, there was no one opposite them. The whole Moosus' army warped simultaneously. The miners did not want to shoot at the people of Moosus. They were grateful to them since they rescued them in the past from the bleak caverns. But their policemen-officers shouted at them and promised each of the young miners a quick execution if they will not continue with the "fight".

Watching the critical situation that developed, Piotr who masqueraded under the name "nick", jumped into the melee and told the other policemen that he will try to convince the miners to fight, but only if they will let him talk to the miners alone and should stay about a mile away. The army of the policemen did not have any ranks, but Piotr, by force of personality, was very respected by both the other policemen and the miners. The policemen-officers discussed the matter among them and complied.

Piotr and the miners moved a mile away and then Peter said: Hyo men! I did not come to persuade you to fight, but just the opposite. I am a rebel, a "fifth columnist." And then he described his life-history to the miners who were overjoyed to hear it. But Piotr silenced them quickly lest some sharp-eyed policeman notice their happiness. He even asked them to put on a sad demeanor, if they can. Then Peter said: "Your company contains 130 men and under only 10 officers. Load you Rifles with one bullet. This is all that you can load at once, as you well know. Now go back slowly and "dejectedly", and when we get to the officers, shoot them like you would shoot mad dogs! The men did just that and moved to other companies one after another. Their training was quite that good. After they moped all the officers, they moved back to Moose's empire and succeeded in killing all Moose's protecting policemen! Those who remained were murderous criminals, but they were cowards too, and they quickly disappeared! The emperor did not know what was happening in his empire since he was closeted in his bedroom with his weekly virgin. Also, he knew that almost all his policemen were busy in the war. But, behind his back all his citizens celebrated !!!

Clark warps to Resurgence (Moose's empire)

Meantime, Moosus planet flourished and received new reincarnateds from Terra. One day Clark was busy meditating for a new immigrant that required an urgent medical help, that the Hospital could not supply. During the medical treatment, one of the Deities spoke to Clark through a loudspeaker that appeared: "Dear Clark. It is against our code to ask you for help, but I must. The population of the large new resurgence is in trouble. Its new name now is "Mooses 'Empire." Moose had become a terrible dictator instead of his prior sweet and generous self. It is not really his fault: His brain underwent a transformation of which he is not aware. The left Carotid artery in his neck, that together with the right-hand carotid sends blood to the brain, developed an occlusion called Atherosclerosis which clogs and stops the flow of blood to the brain. This damaged in his brain the Parietal cortex and the amygdala and turned him from "Dr Jekyll" into "Mister Hyde". Unfortunately, we cannot interfere because we owe him for our past liberation. only you, who also worked in our liberation, can help!"

Very disturbed and unhappy, Clark convened his council, which was his old counseling committee, and he discussed with them a plan to stop Moose, their erstwhile leader.

Once The council conceived a plan, they warped at night to Mooses' Empire - straight to big room that was situated near Moose' elegant bedroom. Moose was fast asleep. Several strong men from Clark's group attacked him and in spite his big bulk, managed to tie him. They also inserted a large piece of cotton wool in his mouth all the way through his throat. This was meant to prevent him from addressing a deity for help. Moose tried to groan and could not. Finally, he cried with tears, to ask for pity.

During the tying operations, one person warped to the

armory, and with the help of their Deity, disposed all the contents of the armory to the sea around the planet. However, they still kept one Thompson gun that they brought to Clark.

Clark told moose that he is very sorry that Moose had become a cruel dictator and also said that his erstwhile council judged him and found him guilty of the death of many young miners. Clark explained to Moose about his Carotid that turned him into a malicious tyrant. He asked moose to pray silently to God for forgiveness. Three minutes later he sadly executed Moose. He had to shoot the whole magazine.

Clark knew Latin. Looking at the dead moose with tears in his eyes, like moose had in his eyes, he quoted a well-known saying: "Sic Transit Gloria Mundi". Clark did not know that Moose had already used this saying in the past when most of his people betrayed him in the earth-like planets, just like Clark now.

The end

Printed in the United States
by Baker & Taylor Publisher Services

Printed in the United States
by Baker & Taylor Publisher Services